Sabine Picout

Doris Lessing, The Golden Notebook - an analysis

GRIN Verlag

Bibliografische Information der Deutschen Nationalbibliothek:

Die Deutsche Bibliothek verzeichnet diese Publikation in der Deutschen National-
bibliografie; detaillierte bibliografische Daten sind im Internet über http://dnb.d-
nb.de/ abrufbar.

Imprint:

Copyright © 2004 GRIN Verlag GmbH
Druck und Bindung: Books on Demand GmbH, Norderstedt Germany
ISBN: 978-3-656-12825-0

This book at GRIN:

http://www.grin.com/en/e-book/188974/doris-lessing-the-golden-notebook-an-
analysis

GRIN - Your knowledge has value

Der GRIN Verlag publiziert seit 1998 wissenschaftliche Arbeiten von Studenten, Hochschullehrern und anderen Akademikern als eBook und gedrucktes Buch. Die Verlagswebsite www.grin.com ist die ideale Plattform zur Veröffentlichung von Hausarbeiten, Abschlussarbeiten, wissenschaftlichen Aufsätzen, Dissertationen und Fachbüchern.

Visit us on the internet:

http://www.grin.com/

http://www.facebook.com/grincom

http://www.twitter.com/grin_com

The Golden Notebook by Doris Lessing

The Golden Notebook was published in 1962 and is one of the best known of
Doris Lessing's novels.

Summary:
The central figure of *"The Golden Notebook"* is Anna Wulf, a writer from
South Africa, living in London. During World War II Anna marries a German
refugee Max but divorces and then emigrates to London with her daughter
Janet. She has a long love affair with Michael and an intense friendship with
Molly.
Being about thirty Anna is in a life crises, disillusioned by communist politics
under Stalin, doubting herself and her literary career. Therefore she needs the
treatment of a psychotherapist. To get things straightened out with herself she
deals with them in four independent notebooks, each one has a different
colour.

Soziopolitical context and main ideas:
As the following part will prove *The Golden Notebook* shows features of a
political novel as well as characteristics of a novel of ideas and has, besides
this, various autobiographic traces.
Racism is not a central topic in *The Golden Notebook* but the problem is
mentioned when the protagonist, Anna, talks about her successful novel
"Frontiers of War" which concerns race relations and forbidden love in
southern Africa.
Doris Lessing escaped from this colonial society to London like Anna. There
she was confronted with the effects of the Cold War in the 1950s which are
mentioned in the novel just as the dangers of nuclear threats are.
Doris Lessing and Anna were both deeply involved in **politics** and together
with most of their friends they became members of the Communist Party. But
trials and atrocities in the Soviet Union and other communist countries or
revelations about Stalin's crimes made them develop a feeling of doubt and
disappointment towards **Communism** which was why they broke with
communism.
Besides this *The Golden Notebook* is about **feminism**. Although Lessing
herself claimed in the preface to the book: "This novel was not a trumpet for
Women's Liberation…", her friends called it "a tract about the sex war".
Anna and Doris Lessing being divorced with a child symbolize "a completely
new type of woman" because they "lead what is known as free lives, that is,
lives like men."
Anna refuses to accept the roles traditionally imposed on women by society.
By describing troubled relationships throughout the novel the author shows
women's dissatisfaction with men.

Another important characteristic feature which slips into Lessing's novel repeatedly is the new way of treating psychological problems. Anna undergoes repeatedly psychotherapy and sees her psychotherapist nicknamed "Mother Sugar". In the course of her treatment the interpretation of her dreams is very important which shows us the influence of Freud and especially of C.G. Jung with his theory of **psychoanalysis**.

A central theme in *The Golden Notebook* are Anna's doubts about the meaningfulness of **literature**.

Structure, time scheme and interpretation (chart of the action):

Doris Lessing wanted to leave behind the form of the conventional realistic novel. Therefore she chose such an extraordinary construction.

The skeleton is the short novel "Free Women" which could stand for itself and is some kind of frame story which is divided into five sections by four notebooks. The notebooks are told by Anna Wulf the main figure of Free Women (each notebook focusing on a different kind of experience).

The <u>Black Notebook</u> is about Anna's time in South Africa and about her best seller "Frontiers of War".

The <u>Red Notebook</u> reports about Anna's political views and her attitudes towards the Communist Party.

The <u>Yellow Notebook</u> contains "The Shadow of the Third" – a manuscript of a novel about a married man and his mistress. It deals indirectly with Anna's five-year relationship with Michael which Lessing projects onto Ella and Paul two fictional characters.

The form of the novel is of immense importance and underlines and reflects the novel's meaning.

Anna's split personality corresponds to the formal fragmentation. The protagonist is imbalanced because she sees each aspect of her life separately. She looks for an equilibrium within her personality. This can only be achieved by giving up writing in her notebooks and by beginning a new one-*The Golden Notebook*, which gives the novel its title. In bringing together her different experiences a certain unity comes into existence which helps to regulate her imbalance in her consciousness.

This turning point in her life has been brought about by the painful but very intense affair with Saul Green. Saul being in the same mental state helps her to regain her personality and individual stability. Based on this experience she can build up a new relation to reality. As soon as she has got over her personal crisis then she has overcome her writer's block.

In Lessing's novel a very complex time scheme can be noted.
The notebooks are written over the same period of time- between 1950 and
1957. But the author does not necessarily stick to a chronological order of the
events in these notebooks because she sometimes changes the sequence of
events. (Futher details **p. 3f.**)
Anna Wulf being a writer herself takes the role of Doris Lessing and
comments instead of her.
In the notebooks Anna Wulf tells her experience in the first person whereas
the same Anna Wulf tells her life in the third-person in the novel "Free
Women". Thus Lessing removes the distinction between fiction and truth.

Bibliography:
- Lessing, Doris: The Golden Notebook. Paladin Grafton Books, London
  Glasgow, 1990
- Fahim, S. Shadia: Doris Lessing. Sufi Equilibrium and the Form of the
  Novel. St. Matin's Press, New York, 1994
- Cheng, Yuan-Jung: Heralds of the Postmodern. Madness and Fiction in
  Conrad, Woolf, and Lessing. Peter Lang, New York, 1999
- Taylor, Jenny: Notebooks/memoirs/archives. Reading and Rereading
  Doris Lessing. Routledge & Kegan Paul, Boston, 1982
- Danziger, Marie A.: Text/Countertext. Postmodern Paranoia in Samuel
  Beckett, Doris Lessing, and Philip Roth. Peter Lang, New York , 1996
- Sprague, Claire: In Pursuit of Doris Lessing. Nine Nations Reading. The
  Macmillan Press, London, 1990
- Kaplan, Carey/Rose, Ellen Cronan: Approaches to Teaching Lessing's
  The Golden Notebook. The Modern Language Association of America,
  New York, 1989
- Seiler-Franklin, Carol: Women in the fiction of Margaret Drabble, Doris
  Lessing, and Iris Murdoch. Peter Lang, Bern, 1979

Structure of the novel:

> *"The two women were alone in the London flat"*

Summer 1957-Anna re-meets Molly

about Molly's husband Richard, his wife Marion, their unhappy marriage

flashback: how Molly and Richard met

Molly occupations: dancing, drawing lessons, actress, journalist

Molly's son (Tommy), Richard's attempts to find a constructive place for him

first doubts about communism.

Flashback: when Anna met Michael (lived with him from 1949-1954)

1951 ??? Anna and agent discussing the making of a film **"Frontiers of War"**

1952 discussion about cast for this film

1953 Memories about African time …about RAF

Novel Reviews

Flashback: end of African period after the war, about weekends with communist group (Paul, Jimmy, Ted, George, Willy, Maryrose…)

January 1950 …February 1950….Communist Party

August 1951 Michael dropped in

September 15th Hungarian Trial

January 3rd 1952 friends of Michael hanged in Prague, Rosenbergs electrocuted

Stalin's death

Julia and Ella working for a women's magazine

Ella writing novel about suicide

Ella's son Michael…

party at Dr. West's house…

Ella about her ex-husband George

About her affair with Paul (a married doctor) - does not want to abandon his wife and his two children…leaves Ella

looking at Ella's affair with Paul Anna realizes what has happened to her and Michael

Ella's statements about orgasm

Commentary to the sociogram:
Now I want to have a quick look at the different characters of this novel and
show how they interrelate.
I am going to start with the characters of "The Shadow of the Third" a mise-
en-abyme novel written into the Yellow notebook.
Ella is the divorced wife of **George** with whom she has a son called **Michael**.
She has an intense affair with the married physician **Paul** Tanner and an
enriching friendship with **Julia**. They are all counterparts of the characters of
The Golden Notebook itself.

We hear about **Anna**'s husband **Max**, leader of the political group in Africa, a
cold and doctrinaire German refugee, whom she divorced after the war and
with whom she had a daughter, called **Janet**.
Janet leaves for boarding school when she is twelve. (She gave Anna's life an
outer shape and afterwards "An Anna is coming to life that died when Janet
was born.")
Like Ella, Anna has a close relationship with a woman friend, **Molly**.
And she has two lovers, first **Michael**, and then **Saul Green**.
When Anna reflects on the events that took place in Africa (at the Mashopi
Hotel...) we hear about the members of the left-wing political group made up
of English airman and local white activists in Africa during World War II...
like **Paul, Willy, Maryrose**...

Molly's ex-husband **Richard** is a failure in private life but a mogul of British
industry. He is unhappily married, to **Marion**, who has drinking problems and
is rejected by Richard.
Tommy, Richard's son from his first marriage to Molly, suffers from
depression and decided to become a conscientious objector. He blinds himself
when trying to shoot himself. After his attempted suicide he moves in with his
step-mother, Marion.

Anna begins a brief affair with the American, **Saul** (called **Milt** in "Free
Women 5").
Saul is an American drop-out with several nervous breakdowns behind him.
Anna takes over his emotions, goes "right inside his craziness". Anna presents
her Golden Notebook to Saul with the first sentence of his novel.
At the point Saul and Anna state "we can't either of us ever go lower than
that" they are able to start at the beginning ...and then return to sanity.
Then Saul sees himself and Anna as part of the "team that haven't given in".

Stylistic Analysis:

It was impossible for me to choose one "key" text extract in order to show characteristic stylistic features of this novel. Doris Lessing has used different kinds of writing and various styles.

Styles change when she refers to other works of fiction like "Frontiers of War" or "The Shadow of the Third" or Saul Green's novel about the Algerian soldier or when she writes various numbered ideas for stories and novels. There are letters, book reviews, newspaper clippings all in different styles.

"A description of her meeting with Joyce, as recorded in the Red Notebook, reveals that pattern in epitome: '*this evening had dinner with Joyce, New Statesman circles, and she started to attack Soviet Union. Instantly I found myself doing that automatic-defence-of Soviet-Union act, which I can't stand when other people do it. She went on; I went on. For her, she was in the presence of a communist so she started on certain clichés. I returned them. Twice tried to break the thing, start on a different level, failed – the atmosphere prickling with hostility.* '"

Especially in the blue notebook where she gives detailed accounts of Anna's life we are confronted with a language typical of diary entries:
"*Jan. 7th, 1950. … Country house. Charming conventional wife. Three delightful little boys. …Richard at home for week-ends, bringing business guests, etc. The local gentry.*"

Talking about the Communist Party or the activities for it she uses typical political jargon.
"*It's all right, comrades, we are going to lose our deposit, we aren't going to win enough votes to split the Labour.*"

And there is the language of feminists:
"*You bring out all this stuff, as if it were the last revelation from some kind of oracle. I bet you talk about sex when you're alone with a popsy. So why put on this club-man's act just because there are two of us?*"

And the language of psychotherapists:
"*The things that are important in life creep up on one unawares, one doesn't expect them, one hasn't given them shape in one's mind. One recognizes them…*"

Often there are only words used to write down certain associations:
"*Men. Women. Bound. Free. Good. Bad. Yes. No. Capitalism . Socialism. Sex. Love…*"